The Three Words

Sai Sindhu Zaddu

BookLeaf
Publishing

Presentation by *BookLeaf Publishing*

Web: www.bookleafpub.com

E-mail: info@bookleafpub.com

ISBN: 9789357695893

First edition 2022

This book is dedicated to those who have been brave enough to walk away from toxicity and those in need of a shoulder to lean on, courage to move on and support to get on.

A Simple Girl

A quiet moment with you under the blanket of
stars,
a happy morning with you next to my heart,
a tight hug with your love, wholeheartedly,
a bright smile on your face every time you look
at me.

I want to be the one who makes you laugh,
the one to whom you pour your heart out
and the one to hold you when you fall.
I want to walk with you through the darkness
and save you from the monsters that you are
better off without.

We can sing, laugh, dance and cry.
We will be what we needed all this time.
I am just a simple girl looking for love
who embraces the little things like a kiss with a
hug.

The Perfect One

I felt like myself from the very second we met.
Never thought I needed to be over-conscious
like elsewhere.
You made everything seem easy, even the smile
that I have been hiding for quite a while.

I would do anything to save this.
Meaning - adjusting and understanding more
than it needs.
I would be happy to be the best friend you got.
Meaning - going to be there whenever you want.

For some reason, all this has been so special.
I am more than glad to have felt this ever.
Not everything needs time to get built and be
perfect,
some things are already found flawless.

Hand Over Heart

My heartbeat was catching up with the bike,
as I leaned on you on that rainy night ride.

My heart melts each time I wake up next to you,
as I see your beautiful face resting with a calm
smile that's so pure.

My heart blushes every time you look at me,
as I know what your eyes want to say to me.

You are an anchor that can calm my heart down
and an earthquake that can shake my whole
world up.
You are my strength and weakness,
and I am willing to risk it all, knowing you will
hold my hand through the darkness.
You are the reason I now know that love is alive.
You will be in my heart until it ceases to exist in
all lives.

Forever In Time

I feel you more than ever, my happiest place.
We were not so sure yet did it at our own pace,
anyways.
It was not unicorns and pearls ever since,
but, now it all makes sense how we are meant to
be.

Do you feel the same way, too?
Did you know what butterflies are because of
me, too?
You are more than a friend and mean more than
family,
you were always there even when you did not
have to be.

My mind says the same as my heart says to me,
to never leave your side through the highs and
the seas.
I can never afford to lose you,
as you are my endgame as I am to you

You have always wanted the best for me,
and brought out the best in me, my best man.
You are the love of my life, forever in time.

Never Without You

I have been through our worst and seen our best.
I have been to the highs and lows and the
in-betweens.
I am constantly reminded of all the broken
times.
I am constantly reminded of all the golden
pieces.

With you, it doesn't matter how it is around me.
With you, it doesn't matter where I am gonna be.
With you, all the broken times are totally worth
it.
With you, it will always be as golden as it can
be.

As days went by, I realised how irreplaceable
our connection is.
As months went by, I felt how pure what we
have is.
As years went by, I knew how inevitably forever
we have become to be.

Beautiful Unplanned Mistake

I never imagined I would be on the other side
I never knew how it would feel to give in once
in a while
I always pictured it to be perfectly fun and
loving
I always thought we would be together in this
until the end.

Now, I see how it kills to have to walk away.
Now, I know how suffocating it is to get nothing
back my way.
Now, I realise that it was just about the fun.
Now, I understand that there never was us.

The Broken Heart

What have I done?
What is wrong this time?
Loving you, loving myself, being loved,
everything feels wrong.

Why is it so hard?
Why should everything be so hard?
playing nice, keeping my cool, staying calm,
everything feels hard.

What do I do now?
How should I know that?
When I am not myself but more of a depressed
loner,
who is to know that?

How could I have known that
love and disappointment are never apart?
How would I have learnt
that this ends with a broken heart?

Who should have told me
that true love goes down taking me along?
How should I know how to deal with this,

when I am dying every minute as the moments'
pass?

It was all beautiful when there were no
expectations,
but with love came more responsibilities and
rejections.
They consumed all the time, and there was none
left for love,
so it started to fall apart, making the suffering
seem a lot.

Happiness is hard to find, and so is the truth.
"Finding your true love is not just enough.
 Finding your peace is underrated as ever. "
Someone should have told this to me as I am
telling it to you.

Now I Know

Sometimes we see through the signs.
Omens are ignored most of the time.
Good or bad, we don't mind if they don't favour
us.
Well, now I know why it rained that night with
heavy clouds.

So How Long?

How long has it been
since you wholeheartedly told me that you love
me?
since you wanted to be forever with me?
since you felt that there could be no one better
for you than me?

How long will it be
before you tell me you want me?
before you realise you are losing me?
before you miss me, noticing it is not the same
me?

How long do I wait
to see us smile with the purest hearts?
to believe that we are going to work no matter
what?
to understand that you would never want to
leave me at any cost?

Will you ever want to show me that you love
me?
Will you ever want to kiss me because you
missed me?

Will you ever want to tell me how much I mean
to you?
If yes, how long do you think it will take you?

The Toxic Love

Did everything I can,
gave everything you want,
a lot of empathy and a lot more love,
more than you ever want.

Wanted you to do the same,
wanted you to stay close to me.
You never really understood it.
You just think you do but never did.

You were good, and you were bad.
Ignored the latter and messed up my life.
Never knew how easy it was
to hate oneself after loving for quite a while.

I deserve more, and maybe you do too.
We just don't fit in anymore and it feels
unacceptable.
But that doesn't make it untrue and
you would agree with this too.

I am done now, and I am done here.
Cared too much for the heart, and my mind is
dying now.

I need to stop this soon and find a way out right
now.
But my heart knows nothing about giving up on
the toxic love.

You Think So?

Do you know how much she loved you?
Did you see her eyes when she looks at you?
Have you ever felt the warmth and the affection
she had for you?
Do you think you and her can feel it all now too?

Did you not know your once stable and strong
girl?
Don't you think it's a far shot for this pathetic
girl?
Do you think you can pull her back together?
Have you not had enough of this?
How can she believe that you want to do this?

Can you cut through her insecurities?
Can you glue her love back together with no
boundaries?
Can you make her feel loved and less alone?
Can you do that? Do You think so?

May be Then

All the sparks and smiles,
all the promises to each other,
Where did it all go now?
All the fights and cries
are all that we are left with now
How did it come to this? How?

I wish you could see how sorry I am
for the way this all turned out to be now.
I wish you could feel how hollow I am,
for the way nothing is all we are left with now.

I hope to see you happy and satisfied someday.
I hope you remember that all I got was you back
in the day.
I hope you know that we did all that we could to
stay.

I feel we will have our forever, the next time.
Maybe then, love will find us and spark a smile.
Maybe then we can have it all and be all we
want.
And, maybe then I can be your always as you
were mine.

Until the next life.

The Missing Piece

I drank till I felt numb, and tried crying my eyes
out,
neither he nor she could make me feel distant
from us.
Joining the pieces with gold seems like a deceit
to me,
as hope is hard to find while I try to fill these
gaps you left within.

The warmth of your touch that fire can not beat,
the life within you that water can not drown,
the wind reminds me of you tucking my hair
back and
you were my constant no matter when,
like the sky is to earth no matter where they are.

You were once everything that I never knew I
needed.
You are now the missing piece in the world I
live in.

I Just Can't

17

I loved you too much to stay now.
I am too blank to pour my feelings out.
I am too shocked at something that I always
knew.
I am too empty to even feel the emptiness as if
it's new.

Storm of You

One night, I sat on our bench silently
with voices inside my head screaming
uncontrollably,
until a gust of wind knocked me out of the
memories.

I am on my side of the bed
wanting to think about anything but the space
next,
while the rain on the window sings as I lay still.

You were once the gale that reminded me to
breathe
and the sound that sang me to sleep.
Now, you are the storm that tears me down from
within.

The Faded Stardust

Your touch was the golden dust that held me
high in the sky.
Your smile was an ember that brightened my
whole life.
My addiction to you was a darkness that clouded
my mind.
My affection for you was ample, heavying my
heart by the end of time.

Our love was sweet with a bond that was
magical.
Indifference became obvious, pushing memories
into oblivion.
We tried our best not to let go of each other
selfishly.
All we were left with was faded stardust,
eventually.

Tale of Us

We were just two lost souls,
searching for love and someone to call our own.
We brought out the worst in each other.
We drained our affection for something that
never even existed.
We tried so hard not to let each other go,
not out of love but because we were scared of
being left alone.

I now see the pattern as I stand back.
There was no way to come out of it with no scar.
Yes, we loved each other very much but
not enough to have a happy ending for this tale
of us.

It was Love

I was not a burden. I was not some
responsibility.
I am sorry you felt that way, but you are wrong
indeed.
I was in love. I was in pain.
I am sorry you did not see it, but none of it was
fake at all like you think.

I wish you had more patience to see me for who
I am.
I wish you held me one last time before you left
home.
However, I think we had a good time and made
memories.
I hope we can cherish it, as I know it was love
that we were in.

The Lost Smile

I started smiling to hide the pain that I was in,
I chose to smile even in the roughest places I
saw myself in,
I had to smile on those days when it felt
impossible.
I smiled, feeling there was nothing else left for
me to say or do.

I slowly grew to know why acceptance is
important.
My smile has now become a constant and not an
act.
I now understand why I should be working
towards myself
because I know this smile can be truer and
brighter even.

I can feel that I am going to be stronger,
I know I have so much more to me than just
being an over-thinker.
I believe there are better days and more love out
there.
I am in search of purpose and happiness and in
love with myself more than yesterday.

The Right Ending

I am doing really great without you in my life.
I am working and being the best self that I
possibly can.
I am doing everything I want to with no regrets.
I am finally with myself like how I always
thought I can.

Sometimes, I miss our conversations and smiles.
I miss our tickle fights and laughter.
We will always be a big part of my life.
For there has been a hell lot of good, to forget us
like we never happened.

I am glad we have known each other and been
there for one another.
I hope you find your happiness and everything
that you wish and fight for.

The Three Words

The past few months have been hard and felt
like hell.
But, there is so much I realised in the end.
There are a lot of three words that are so special,
but these are a few that helped me get through it.

'Don't be afraid' to choose yourself over
negativity. Walk away.
Nothing is worth giving your inner peace and
strength away.

'You have you' to remind yourself of your worth.
Remember that.
As having your people around, to tell you that is
impossible during your every doubt.

'Stand for yourself'. Your flaws, values, mistakes
and power, own it.
Because acceptance is the most necessary truth
of all.

'You know yourself' better than anyone. Decide
wisely.
Forgetting or forgiving may not work every
time, but making peace is important each time.

'You are enough' sounds like a common thing to
say to yourself. But mean it.
As all you want and want to be is within you, so
just breathe.

'I am happy' with where I am in life after so
long.
I am writing to tell you I am in 'love with
MYSELF' after it all.